MEL BAY PRESENTS

FLUID SOLOING

BY TIM QUINN

GW00888764

MBGU • MEL BAY GUITAR UNIVERSITY

BOOK #3 CHORD-LEAD SOLOING FOR GUITAR

CD contents

1 2 3 4 5 6 7 8 9 0

Visit us on the Web at www.melbay.com ó E-mail us at email@melbay.com

<u>a</u>cknowledgements

A heartfelt thanks goes out to all the teachers who profoundly impacted my own playing and learning...thank you Jack Petersen, Dan Haerle, Rich Matteson, and Tom Johnson at the University of North Texas, as well as to my teachers at Berklee College of Music. To the musicians who have been so inspiring...Steve Morse, Pat Martino, John Coltrane, Eric Johnson, Chick Corea, Jimi Hendrix, Frank Zappa, Barney Kessell, Wes Montgomery, Stevie Ray Vaughan, Albert King, Jeff Beck, Steve Vai, Dexter Gordon, Cannonball Adderly, Joe Satriani, Igor Stravinsky, Eddie Van Halen, Al DiMeola, Greg Howe, Joe Pass, Robben Ford, Vinnie Moore, Allan Holdsworth, and Carlos Santana; for the teachings of Paramahansa Yogananda; also to Bill Bay and the fine staff at Mel Bay Publications, Inc.; to Bruce Saunders for his caring engraving; to Dave Austin and George Sanchez for their generous assistance; to Josquin DePres at Track Star Studios for much inspiration and guidance; to the many students who have been indispensable in helping me streamline these materials; to my parents who provided the music education and encouraged the young performer; and especially to my wife, Mari, who lovingly tolerated the thousands of hours with me at the guitar while I formulated these concepts...thank you.

contents

Each example in this book is numbered, referring to the CD Track number.

introduction

Chord-Lead Soloing presents a complete method for developing whole-neck, fluid chord-melody motion using two-string "double-stops", such as in the recordings of guitar legends Curtis Mayfield, Steve Cropper, Jimi Hendrix, Stevie Ray Vaughan, Eric Johnson, and Steve Vai. This style of guitar playing is simultaneously *chordal* (implying a specific major or minor chord), and at the same time *melodic* (carrying a distinct singable melody). This book shows the guitarist how to develop this technique and create continuous connections of moving voicings, merging lead and rhythm guitar into **one flowing melodic chordal texture.**

Hendrix took double-stop chord-melody to an unprecedented level and prominence in the songs "Little Wing", "Castles Made of Sand", "The Wind Cries Mary", and "Electric Ladyland", although he was likely heavily influenced by Mayfield's work with the Impressions (and perhaps Cropper's work with Otis Redding) in developing this aspect of his playing. All three should be acknowledged historically as being among the originators of this style. However, for most of the guitarists who later developed this "chord-lead" style, including Stevie Ray Vaughan, Steve Vai, and Eric Johnson, the primary inspiration was Jimi Hendrix.

Double-stop chord-melody playing can be adapted to every genre of music; whether it's jazz, hard rock, alternative, funk, R&B, country, pop, salsa, reggae, Irish folk, or whatever! Mastering chord-lead technique greatly increases a guitarist's ability to "stand alone"–that is, to play by himself, unaccompanied by any other musicians, mixing and switching between chording and lead improvisation. This is an important, highly sought after skill for the accomplished, professional guitarist. **Chord-Lead Soloing** presents a complete and thorough method for developing this crucial style of playing.

This book is the third book in the **'Fluid Soloing Series'**, a unified set of books that develop different aspects of whole neck fluid motion on the guitar. The three "Comprehensive" soloing etudes at the very end of this book are included to demonstrate some of the techniques from the other three books in the series, as well as the techniques presented in this book, all used in combination. The varied combinations of soloing techniques in these etudes create an exciting whole-neck soloing style that is flowing and varied in its melodic content. If you like the content of this book, check out the other books in the series as well. May you absorb the riches in this book, and may you play beautiful guitar music! Peace and harmony, friends.

section ONE

chord lead basics

"the concept"

This section explains the construction of two-string "double-stops" that are derived from triad shapes and pentatonic scales. "Double-stops" are melodic passages that consist of a series of two note voicings played successively, creating a more chordal way of moving across the fretboard. This type of motion serves as an ideal contrast and compliment to single note melodic improvisation, and is a distinguishing characteristic of Jimi Hendrix's guitar playing style.

the concept of suspension

Every example in this chapter is based on the idea of **"suspension"**, which in strict theoretical terms means <u>replacing the 3rd of a major triad with the 4th</u>. Doing this creates a slight tension in the sound of the chord (hence the term "suspension"), which is resolved when the 4th then goes back to the 3rd of the chord. Listen to this sound when applied to an F major triad, (Ex. 1), replacing the 3rd of the triad, A, with the 4th, B♭:

Ex. 1			Ex. 2			Ex. 3			Ex. 4		
F	F sus⁴	F	F	F⁶	F	F	F(ADD 9)	F	F	F sus²	F

```
T   1   1   1  | 1   3   1  | 1   1   1  | 1   1   1
A   2   3   2  | 2   2   2  | 2   2   2  | 2   0   2
B   3   3   3  | 3   3   3  | 3   5   3  | 3   3   3
```

This concept in tension-resolution can be extended by replacing the 5th, C, with the 6th, D (Ex. 2). Further, the root of the triad, F, or the 3rd, A, can be replaced with the 2nd, G (Ex. 3-4). **This means that each of the three notes in a major triad can be "suspended"**. It is essential for the guitarist to know major triads as they occur on the fretboard, and to understand how to suspend those triads.

important points for study

▸ **Major triads** are presented at the beginning of this chapter in two ways:

1) **Sets 1-3**, the standard 3-note major triad groupings on guitar; and

2) **Sets 1a-3a**, the same triads presented again, but now in two string pairings. While it is logical to memorize the triads in three-note groups, the guitar technique we are developing here uses two strings at a time rather than three, more often than not.

▸ Understand the demonstration on page 9, which shows all of the "suspensions" as applied to triad Set 1a. Again, the four movements that can occur within a major triad (individually or in combination) are:

1) 3 ╱ 4 ╲ 3	3) 1 ╱ 2 ╲ 1
2) 5 ╱ 6 ╲ 5	4) 3 ╲ 2 ╱ 3

▸ Memorize the F major pentatonic scale, and the "fourths" exercises, as presented on page 13. This is an absolute prerequisite for studying this subject.

▸ The licks work equally well for outlining an F major chord [F-A-C], or a Dm7 chord [D-F-A-C]. The F major pentatonic and the D minor pentatonic scales contain the same notes. All the material in this chapter can be applied to F major, or to D minor.

The FIVE key ingredients the guitarist must comprehend in order to master this style of playing are:

❶ Major Triad Sets (in three positions)

❷ Same triad sets seen in two-string pairings

❸ "Suspension" as applied to two-string pairs

❹ Five fingerings for the major pentatonic scale

❺ Same major pentatonic scales played in "fourths"

major triad sets (in 3 positions)

No. I shows the fundamental major triad shapes for an F major triad.
No. 2 shows the same triads played in two-string pairings.

 No. 1 ▸ **Major Triad Shapes (F)**

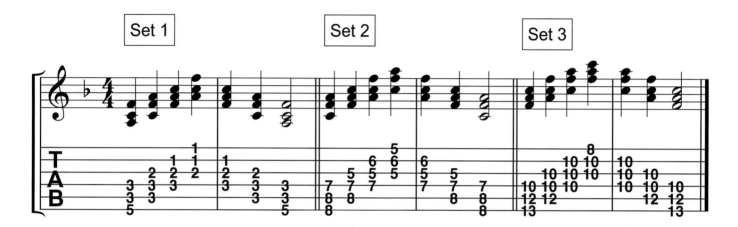

 No. 2 ▸ **Major Triads in 2-String Pairs (F)**

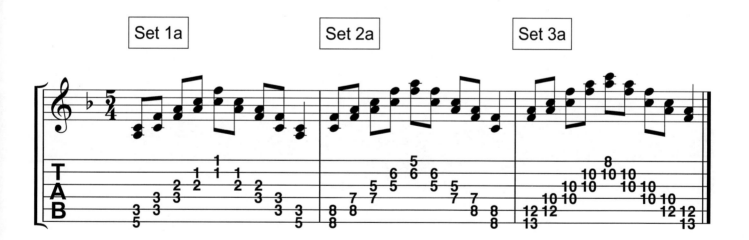

"suspension" applied to 2-string pairs of set 1a

This example demonstrates the possible "suspension" moves as applied to the 2-string pairs of triad Set 1a. (This presentation is offered primarily as a place to examine the theory behind the technique. Examples No. 4-7 present a better way to study isolated "suspension" moves as applied to all of the 2-string triad pairings.)

No. 3 ▶ **Demonstrating possible moves applied to 2-string pairings in one position.**

The material on this page effectively explains the many possible ways to manipulate the major triad with "suspension", even if it might seem somewhat redundant and uninteresting. The knowledge offered here will provide much insight into the construction of the upcoming licks and soloing etudes, and will allow you to master this style more completely (since you will understand it). Take my word for it. Go straight to the licks section if you want to, but do revisit pages 9-13 later for full comprehension.

2-string activity "cells" along the neck

These studies provide a foundation for what lies ahead in the licks. All examples outline an F major chord, but can also be used for D minor.

Fluid chord-melody requires continual movement on the fretboard. These activity cells are like chord-melody "islands", where your hand can land and work out momentarily before floating across the fretboard to a different "island." Each "island" works around an F major triad or the F major pentatonic scale. The movement shown here is simply "suspension" being applied, as described in the previous pages.

Play each measure twice before moving to the next measure.

 No. 4 ▸ **Strings 1 & 2**

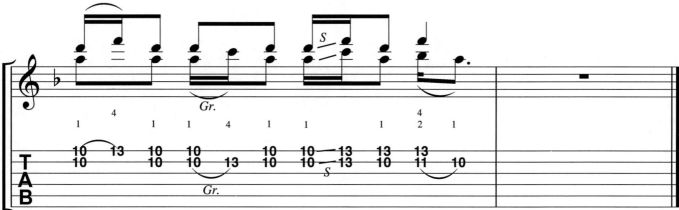

No. 5 ▸ Strings 2 & 3

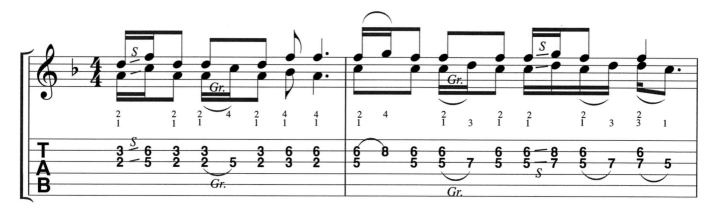

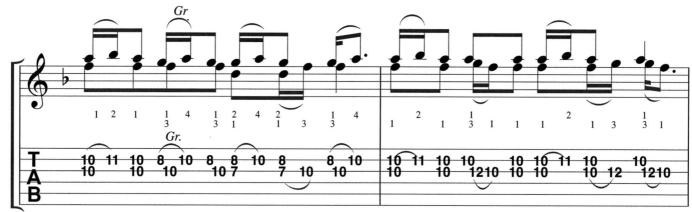

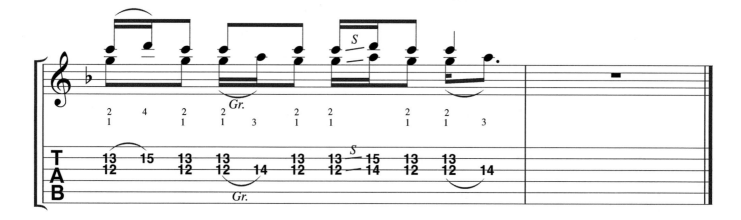

No. 6 ▸ **Strings 3 & 4**

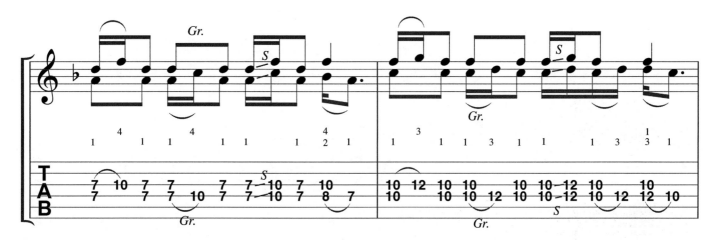

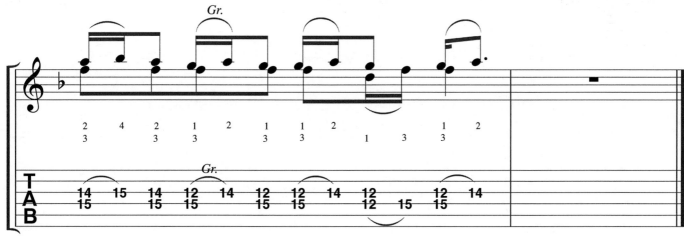

No. 7 ▸ Strings 4 & 5

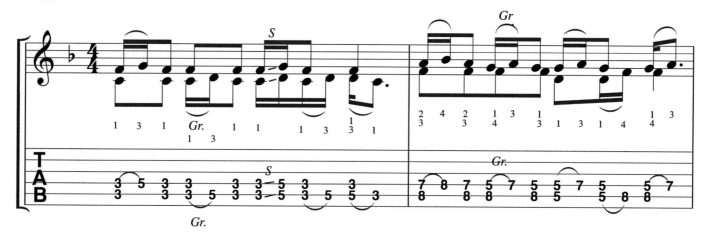

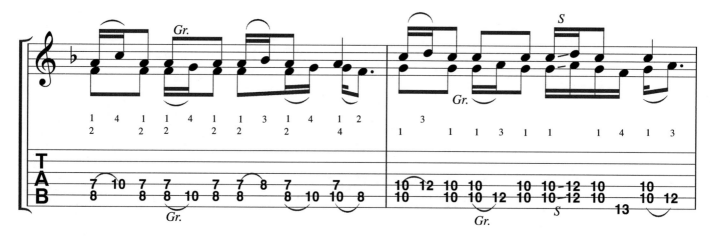

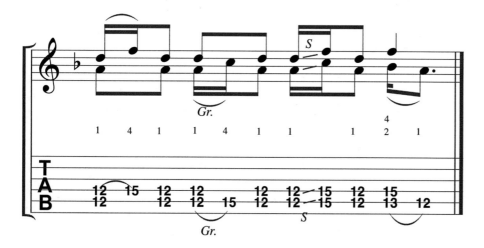

When holding two notes and doing a hammer-on on only one of the two strings, take care not to accidentally deaden the note that is supposed to sustain while the hammer occurs on the other string. This requires the correct left-hand positioning with the thumb lower on the neck and the fingers more parallel to the frets. It is up to the student to assert "quality-control" in playing the material in this book. Frequent accidental deadening of notes takes the magic right out of it! Make sure both notes ring fully when doing a one-string hammer on a two-note shape!!

pentatonic scale in "fourths" (5 fingerings)

Play each fourths exercise repetitively. (Key of: F Major Pentatonic).

Only the first of these exercises is demonstrated on CD track No. 8.

 No. 8 ▸ Fingering 1 in Fourths

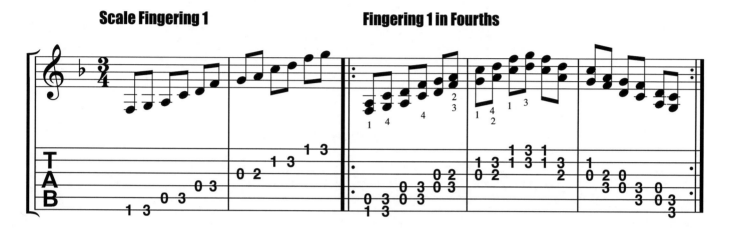

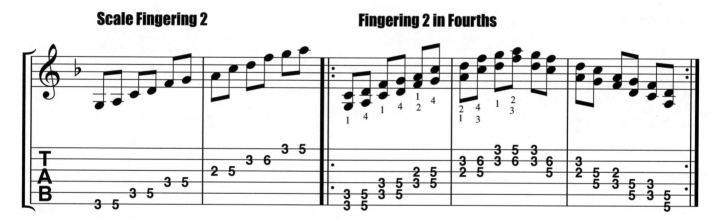

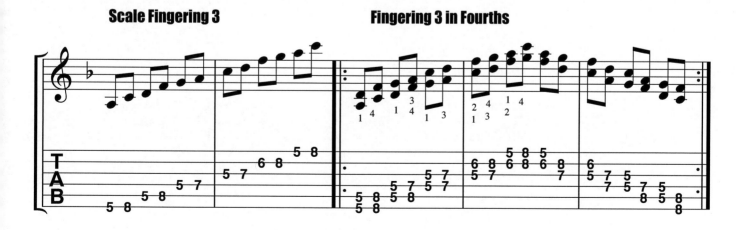

Scale Fingering 4

Fingering 4 in Fourths

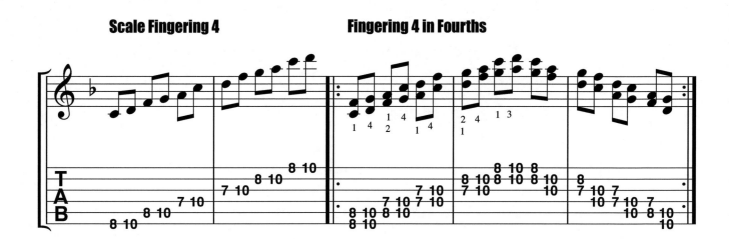

Scale Fingering 5

Fingering 5 in Fourths

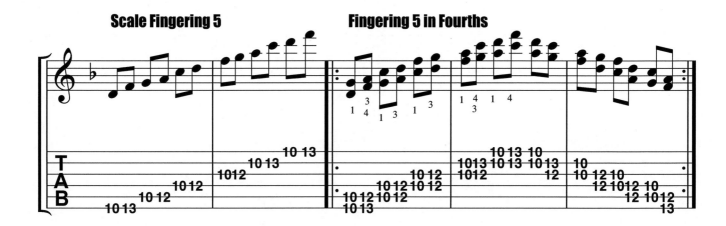

section two

chord-lead licks

This section contains the building blocks for establishing fluid, whole neck motion using chord-melody in the style of Hendrix. Presented here are 15 primary licks, each two measures long. Each lick is presented in three different fingerings, which results in a total of 45 two-measure phrases. Keep in mind, also, that each lick could be broken into two separate licks, each one measure in duration. That would be 90 one-measure ideas for this style of playing. All licks imply the sound of an F major chord (or can also be used to imply the sound of a Dmi7 chord, the relative minor).

Learning all of the licks in this section will result in complete access to every corner of the fretboard using this style of chord-lead. The key to fluidity with this technique is in sustaining constant motion with slides, hammer-ons and pull-offs, continually shifting positions. That is why each lick is presented in three fingerings; knowing multiple fingerings for a given phrase provides a wealth of possible moves, no matter where on the neck your hand may be. When the guitarist has achieved a strong familiarity with all of these chord-melody phrases, his hand can float across the fretboard without having to pause, connecting one idea to another, and then another. The resulting effect is a sound that is rich in texture, simultaneously both chordal and melodic.

Spend sufficient time practicing these licks, and understand the theory behind them. Remember, we are manipulating major triads and working within the major pentatonic scale. If there is a lack of understanding the construction of these licks, spend more time with Section One.

Play all the licks over the following two accompaniment tracks, and try to integrate them into your improvisation. Mix the licks with single-note pentatonic soloing.

No. 9 ▸ Accompaniment Track in F Major

```
      F    Bb        ./.          ./.      F    C  Bb
||: / / / / | / / / / | / / / / | / / / / :||
```

No. 10 ▸ Accompaniment Track in D minor

```
      Dmi   C         ./.          ./.      Bb   C
||: / / / / | / / / / | / / / / | / / / / :||
```

Lick # 1

CD Track No. 11 demonstrates this lick as played in Fingering 2. Play the other fingerings with an identical feel. A slight alteration occurs at the end of Fingering 3. This is necessary in order to play this lick on this string set.

This lick outlines the sound of an F Major chord (or Dmi7).

 No. 11 ▸ **F Major / D minor / Lick # 1**

In the first measure of Fingering 2, a barre at the 10th fret is required. This an excellent place to make the following point: It is the author's suggestion to place the first finger on just two strings at a time, then pick it up and place it on the next two string pair, then pick it up and place it on the next two string pair, instead of barring across the whole fretboard and leaving it down for the entire measure. The resulting sound has better tone and avoids the annoying ringing of previously sounded notes associated with the full-barre approach. This concept should be applied throughout this book.

Lick # 2

CD Track No. 12 demonstrates this lick as played in Fingering 2. Play the other fingerings with an identical feel.

This lick outlines the sound of an F Major chord (or Dmi7).

 No. 12 ▸ **F Major / D minor / Lick # 2**

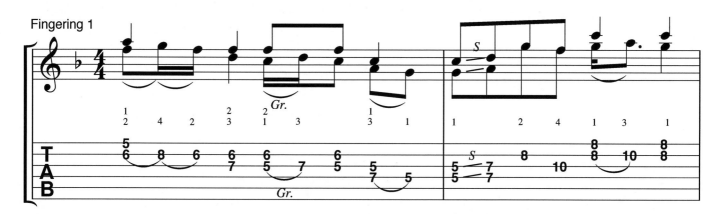

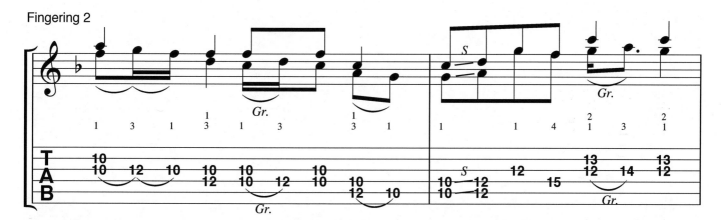

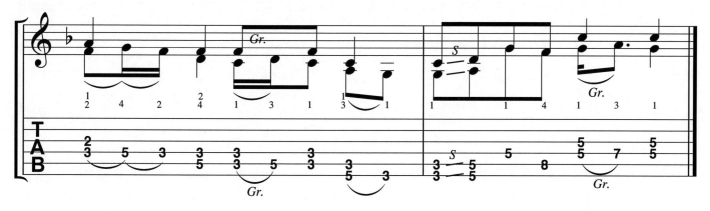

Lick # 3

Outlining the sound of an F Major chord (or Dmi7).

 No. 13 ▸ **F Major / D minor / Lick # 3**

Fingering 1

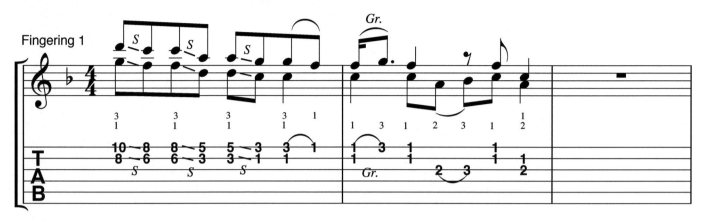

Fingering 2

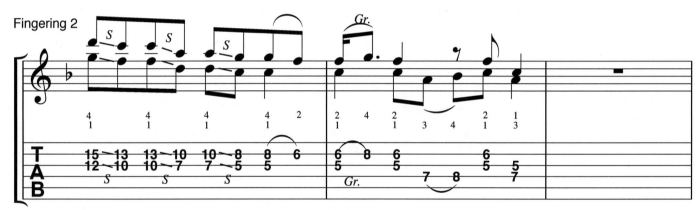

Fingering 3

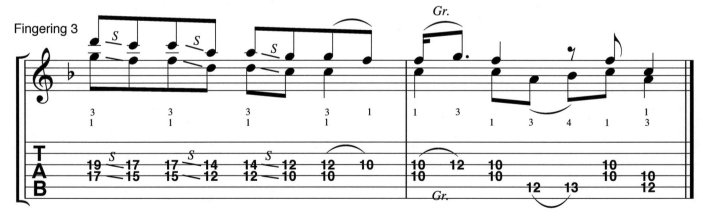

Always listen to the recorded examples on the CD, paying close attention to the articulation of each lick. Occasionally, some aspects of phrasing might not be represented in the notation, but rather left to your ears to discern.

Lick # 4

Outlining the sound of an F Major chord (or Dmi7).

 No. 14 ▸ **F Major / D minor / Lick # 4**

Fingering 1

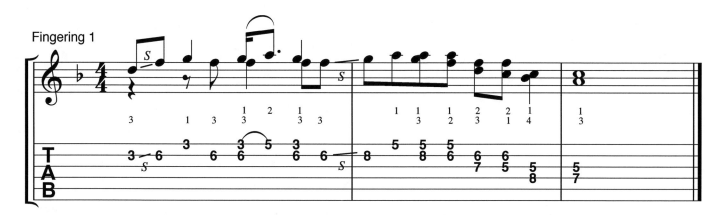

Fingering 2

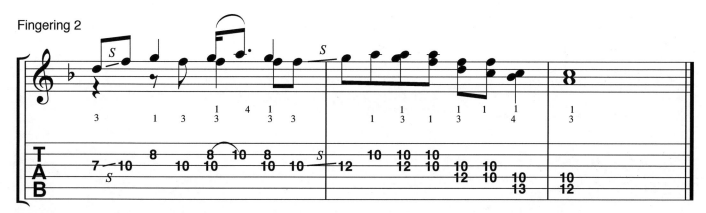

Fingering 3

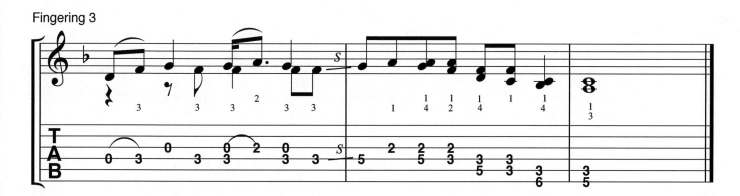

Be sure to try each lick in other keys by moving it up or down the neck, especially licks that use open strings, as in Fingering 3 of this lick. It is important to try this fingering in another key to see how it will be played when open strings are not used.

Lick # 5

Outlining the sound of an F Major chord (or Dmi7).

 No. 15 ▸ F Major / D minor / Lick #5

Fingering 1

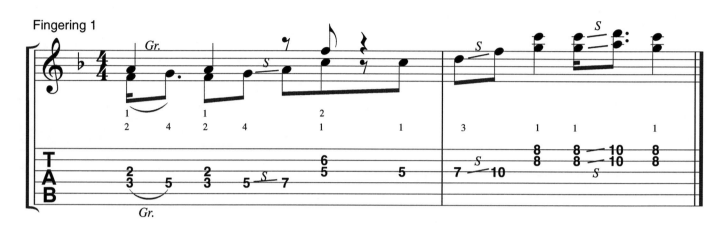

Fingering 2

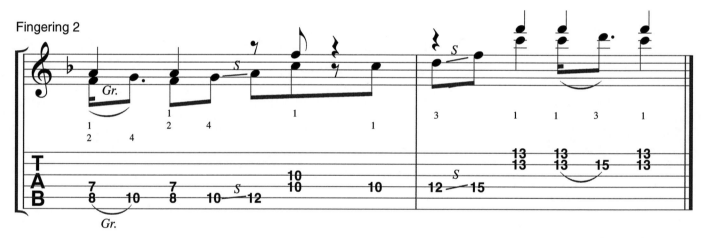

Fingering 3

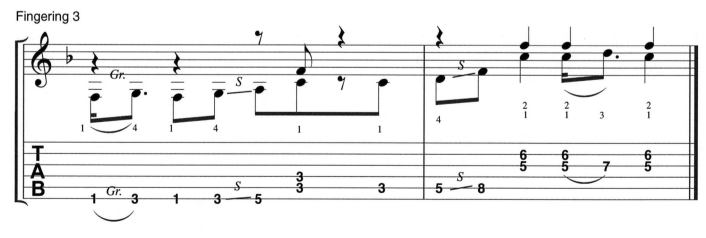

Lick # 6

Outlining the sound of an F Major chord (or Dmi7).

 No. 16 ▸ **F Major / D minor / Lick # 6**

Fingering 1

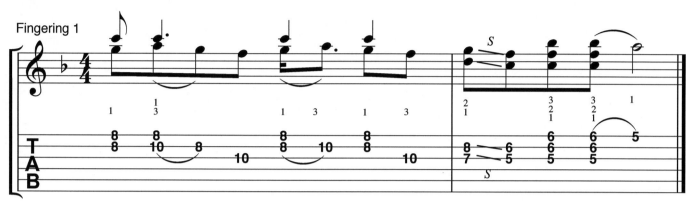

Fingering 2

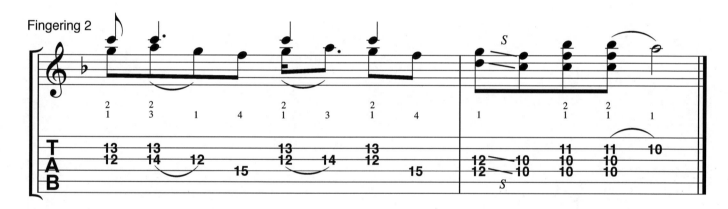

Fingering 3

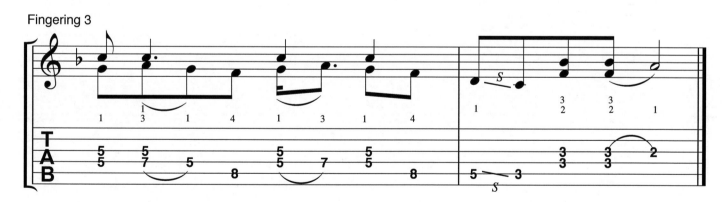

Fingering 4

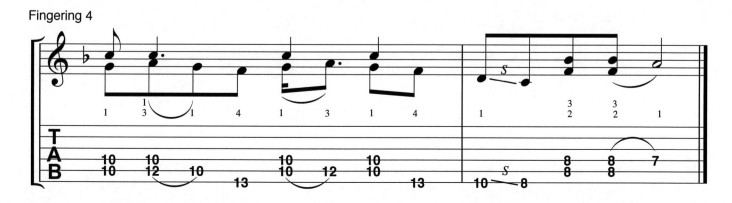

Lick # 7

Outlining the sound of an F Major chord (or Dmi7).

No. 17 ▸ **F Major / D minor / Lick # 7**

Fingering 1

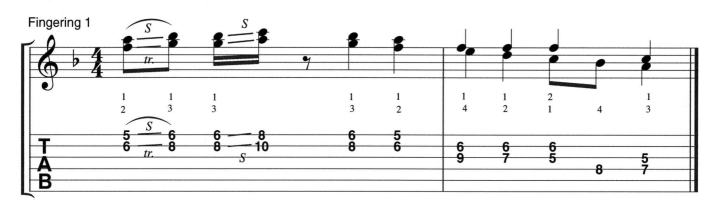

Fingering 2

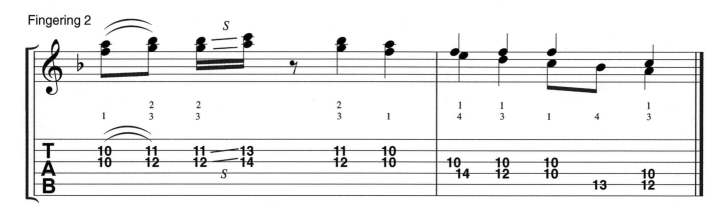

Fingering 3

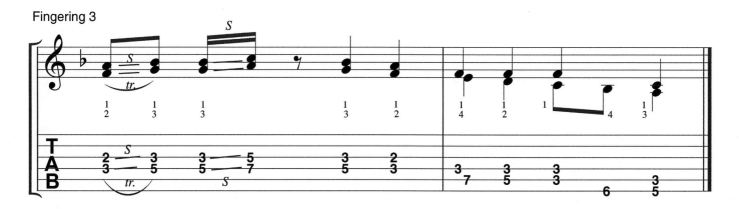

Fingering 4

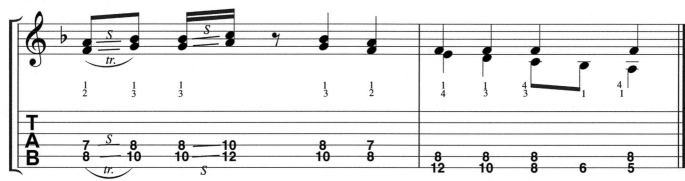

Lick # 8

Outlining the sound of an F Major chord (or Dmi7).

 No. 18 ▸ **F Major / D minor / Lick # 8**

Fingering 1

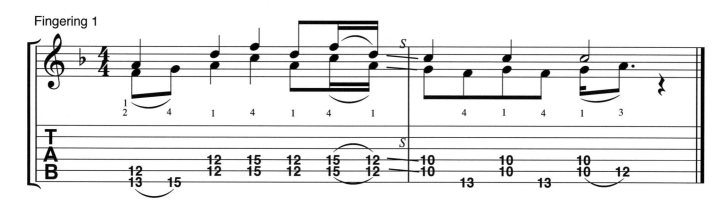

Fingering 2

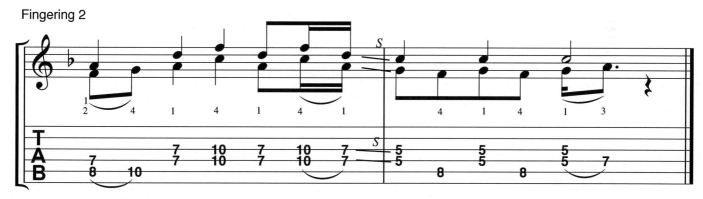

Fingering 3 (note rhythmic phrasing on beat 4 of 1st measure is altered here)

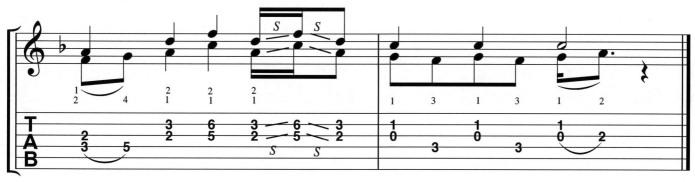

Fingering 4

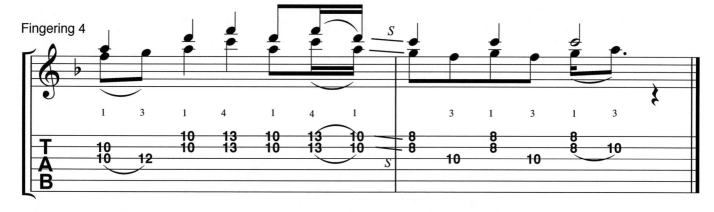

Lick # 9

Outlining the sound of an F Major chord (or Dmi7).

 No. 19 ▸ **F Major / D minor / Lick # 9**

Fingering 1

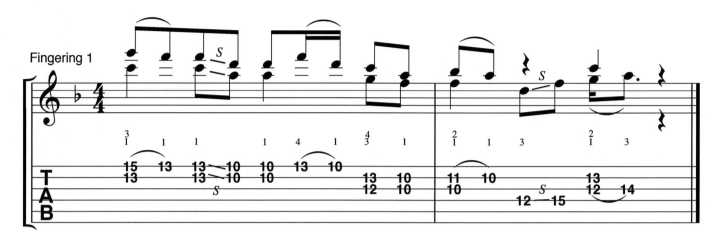

Fingering 2

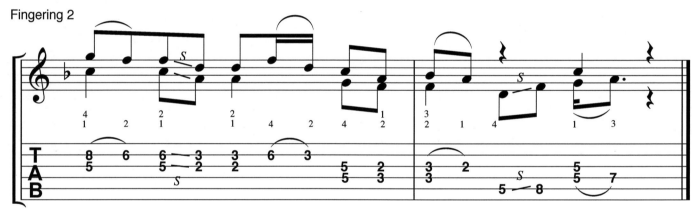

Fingering 3

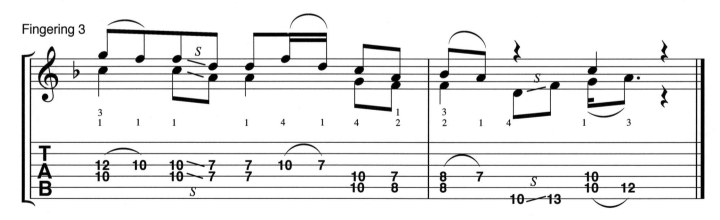

Lick # 10

Outlining the sound of an F Major chord (or Dmi7).

 No. 20 ▸ **F Major / D minor / Lick # 10**

Fingering 1

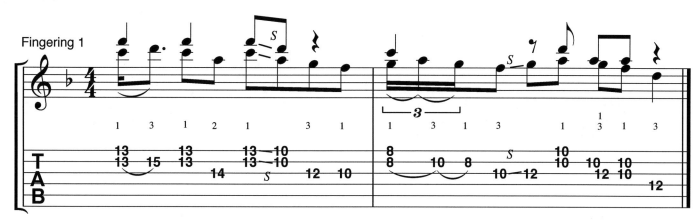

Fingering 2

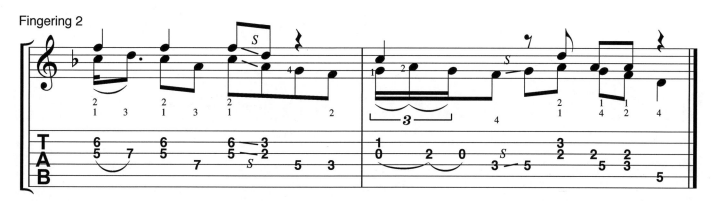

Fingering 3

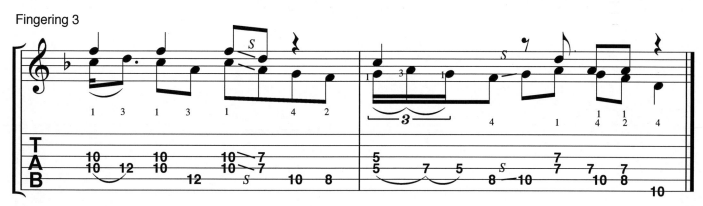

Fingering 4

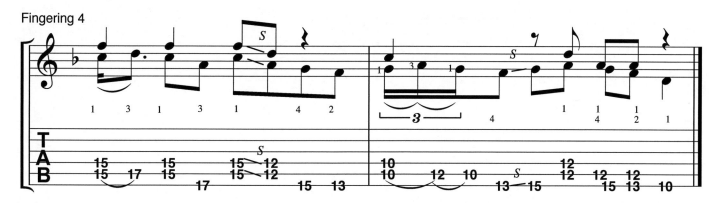

Lick # 11

Outlining the sound of an F Major chord (or Dmi7).

 No. 21 ▸ F Major / D minor / Lick # 11

Fingering 1

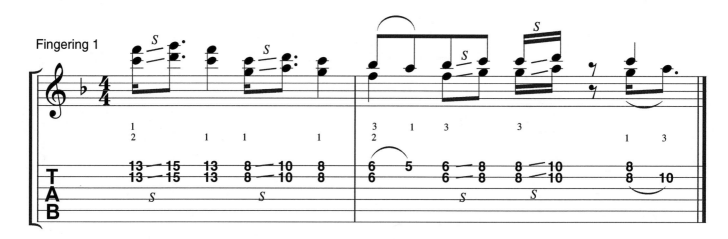

Fingering 2

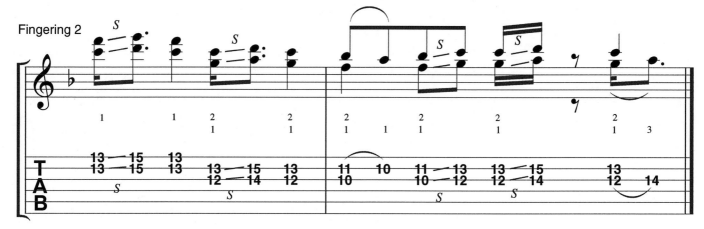

Fingering 3

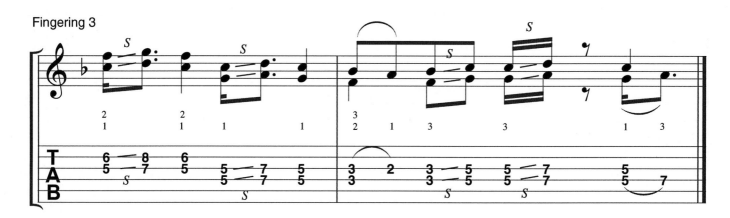

No. 21 (cont.)

Fingering 4

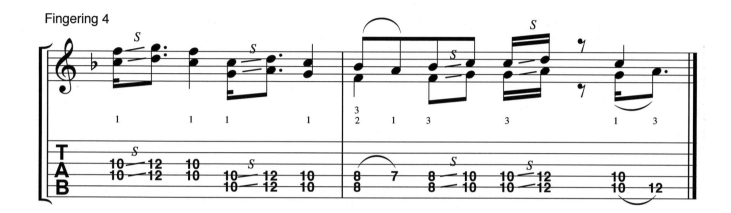

Fingering 5

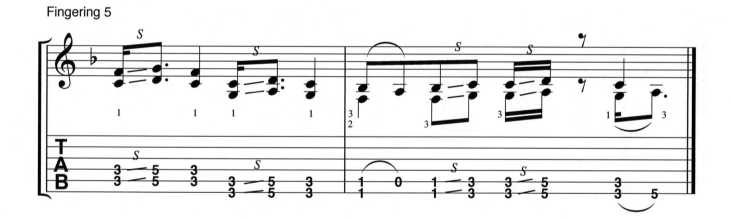

Lick # 12

Outlining the sound of an F Major chord (or Dmi7).

 No. 22 ▸ F Major / D minor / Lick # 12

Lick # 13

Outlining the sound of an F Major chord (or Dmi7).

 No. 23 ▸ F Major / D minor / Lick # 13

Fingering 1

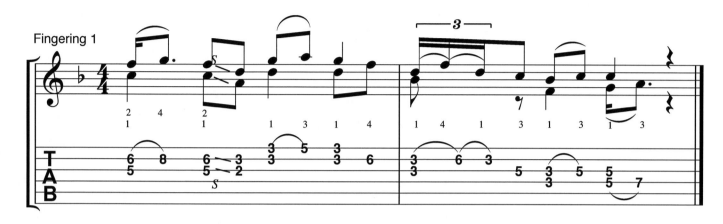

Fingering 2

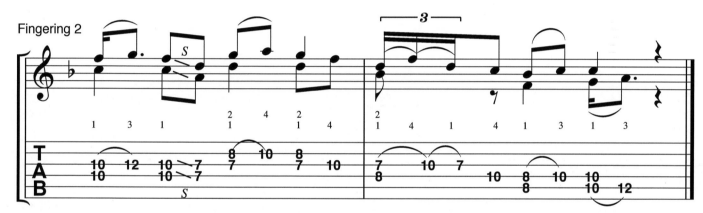

Fingering 3

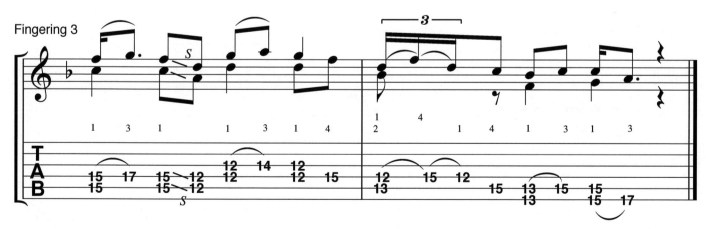

Lick # 14

Although a slide is indicated, a hammer-on may also be used between the first two notes of this lick. Learn both.

Outlining the sound of an F Major (or Dminor).

 No. 24 ▸ **F Major / D minor / Lick # 14**

Important note...

Try all licks in other keys! The licks are presented in the key of F Major/D minor for the purpose of allowing the student to fully grasp the whole neck view. Learning a given concept thoroughly over the entire neck (in a single key) is a smart approach for conceptual assimilation, but there is much work to be done in applying this material to other keys!!

Lick # 15

Outlining the sound of an F Major (or D minor).

 No. 25 ▸ F Major / D minor / Lick # 15

Fingering 1

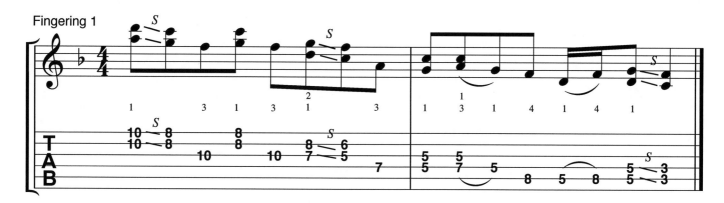

Fingering 2

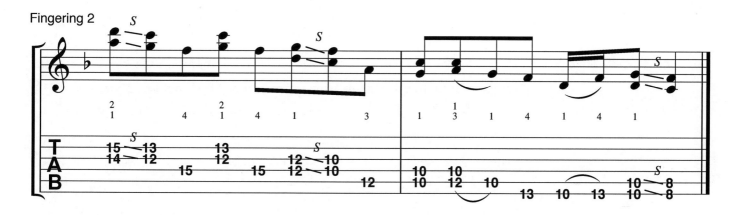

Fingering 3

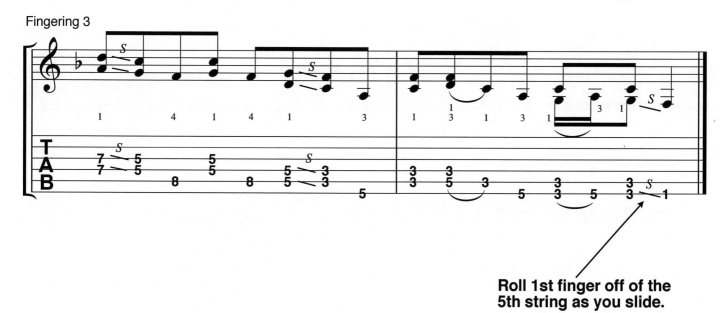

Roll 1st finger off of the 5th string as you slide.

section three

soloing etudes

Soloing Etude No. 1 ▶ This study outlines one chord sound; an F major chord. Alternately, this study could also be seen as outlining a Dmi7 chord instead. This is because the notes of an F major chord [F-A-C] are contained within a Dmi7 chord [D-F-A-C]. So, the student should play this study over BOTH of the backing tracks in F major (CD Track No. 9), and D minor (CD Track No. 10).

Soloing Etude No. 2 ▶ This study is written over a diatonic chord progression in the key of F major. Here, a different approach to using pentatonic chord-melody is presented, where each chord is outlined individually. The F major chord is outlined using F major triads and the F major pentatonic scale, the C major chord is outlined with C major triads and the C major pentatonic scale, the D minor chord is outlined using D minor pentatonic (diatonically, the same as the treatment as that of the F major chord), and the Bb major chord is outlined with Bb major triads and the Bb major pentatonic scale.

Soloing Etude No. 3 ▶ This study combines techniques from this book with Extended Arpeggio Runs from Book 1 in the 'FLUID SOLOING SERIES'. (Key of D major.)

Soloing Etude No. 4 ▶ This study also combines techniques from this book with Extended Arpeggio Runs from Book 1 in the 'FLUID SOLOING SERIES'. (Key of E minor.)

Soloing Etude No. 5 ▶ This study combines techniques from this book with techniques from Books 1, 2, and 4 in the 'FLUID SOLOING SERIES'. (Key of C minor.)

Soloing Etude No. 1

Whole neck study outlining one chord sound (works for an F Major chord or Dmi7).

Play repetitively over CD accompaniment track No. 9 in F Major, as well as over track No. 10 in D minor.

 No. 26 ▸ **F Major (or Dmi7)**

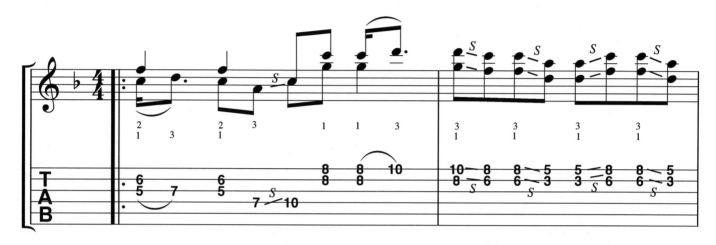

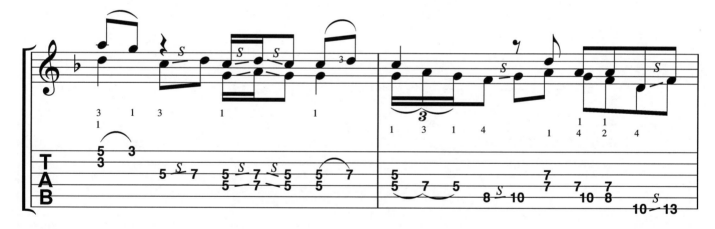

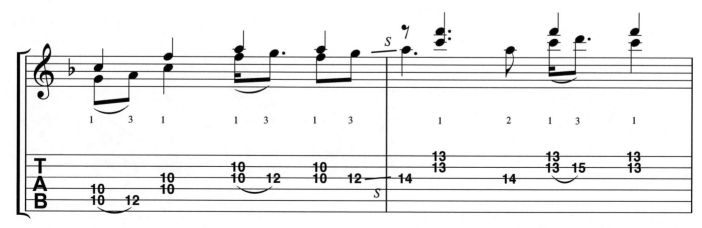

No. 26 ▸ page 2

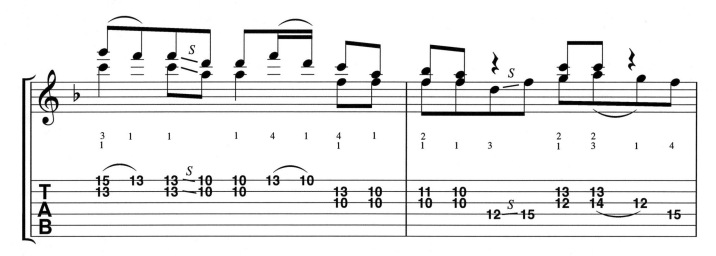

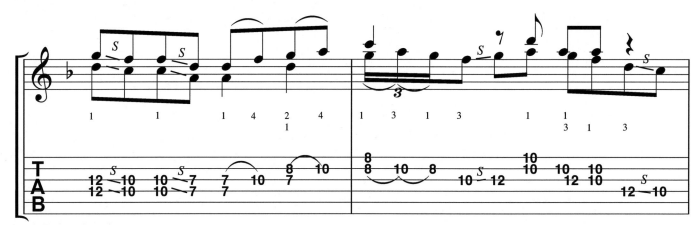

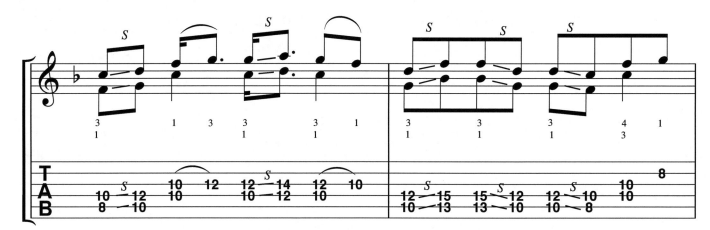

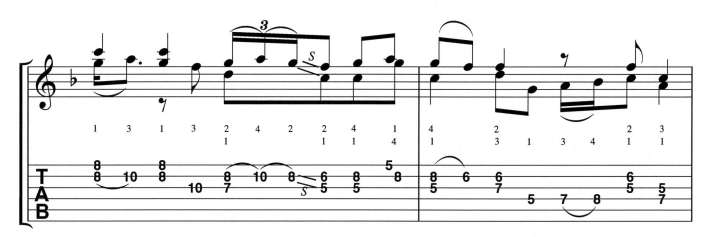

No. 26 ▸ page 3

Soloing Etude No. 2

Study in outlining each chord individually using chord-lead soloing.

Play this study repetitively over the following chord progression: ‖: F | C | Dmi | B♭ :‖
(This study uses F major pentatonic on the F chord, C major pent. on C, D minor pent. on Dmi, and B♭ major pent. on B♭)

No. 27 ▸ **Chord Outlining Etude**

No. 27 ▸ Chord Outlining Etude (cont.)

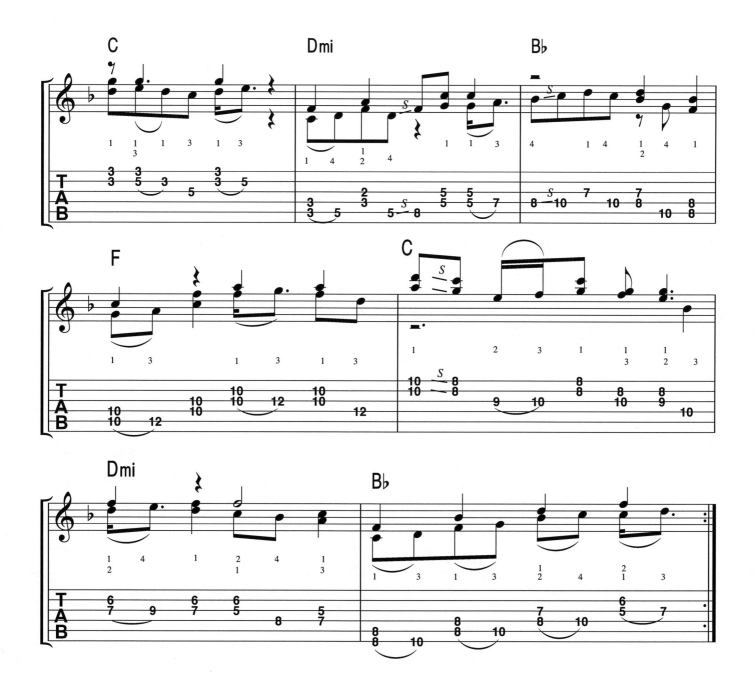

Soloing Etude No. 3 (Comprehensive)

Combining chord-lead motion with major triad arpeggio runs (from Book 1)

Play this study repetitively over the following chord progression: ‖: D G | ⁒ :‖
This study uses the D major pentatonic scale and D major argeggio runs, outlining a D major chord.

No. 28 ▶ **Etude No. 3**

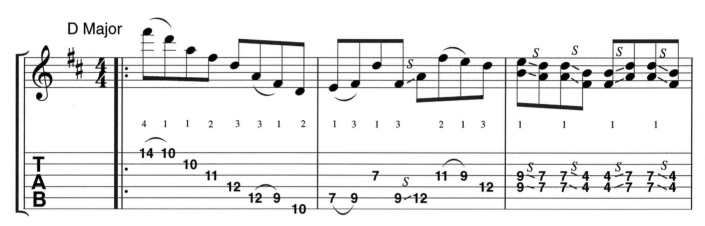

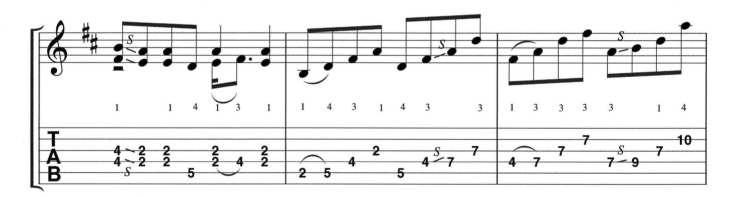

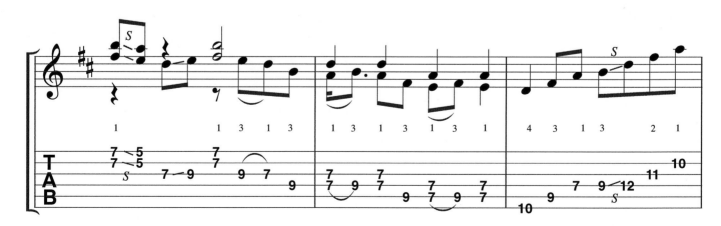

No. 28 ▸ Etude No. 3 (cont.)

Soloing Etude No. 4 (Comprehensive)

Combining chord-lead motion with minor 7th arpeggio runs (from Book 1)

Play this study repetitively over the following chord progression: ‖: Emi │ G │ Ami │ C B7 :‖
All runs and licks outline an Emi7 chord, but work against all chords in the progression (typical of minor pentatonic soloing).

 No. 29 ▸ **Etude No. 4**

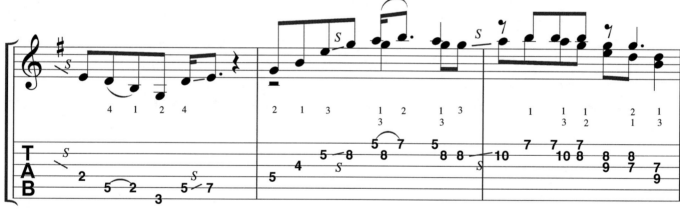

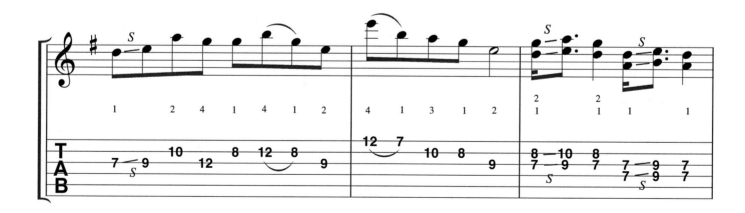

No. 29 ▸ Etude No. 4 (cont.)

Soloing Etude No. 5 (Comprehensive)

Combining techniques from this book and other books in the series, to create fluid motion.

Chord Progression

‖: Cmi7 | ⁒ | Cmi7 | ⁒ | Cmi7 | ⁒ | Cmi7 | ⁒ | B♭ | ⁒ |
|Cmi7 | ⁒ | B♭ | ⁒ | Cmi7 | ⁒ |B♭ A♭| G7 | Cmi7 | ⁒ :‖

No. 30 ▸ Etude No. 5

(Double Pentatonic Shape)

(4 Bar Intro)

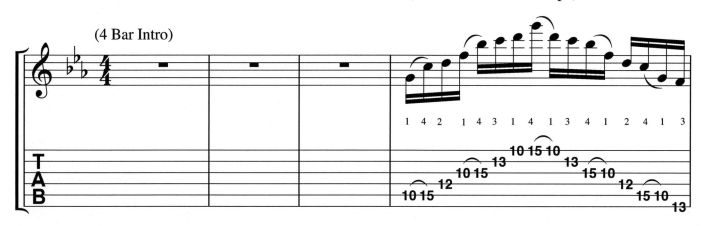

(Horizontal Pentatonic Motion)

Cmi⁷

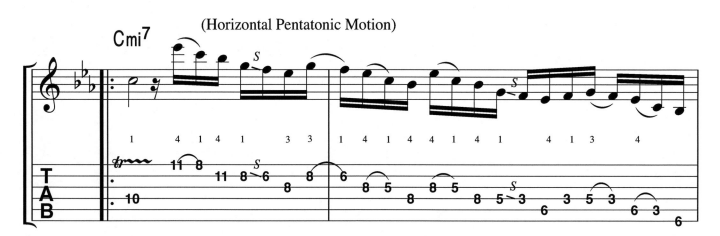

Cmi⁷ (Double Pentatonic Shape)

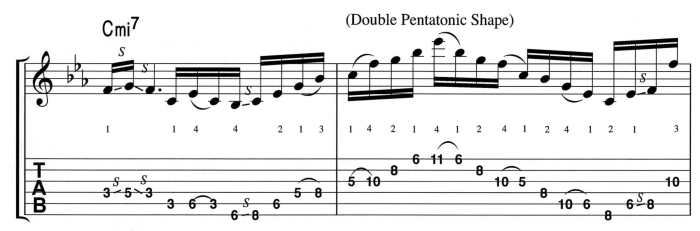

No. 30 ▸ Etude No. 5 (cont.)

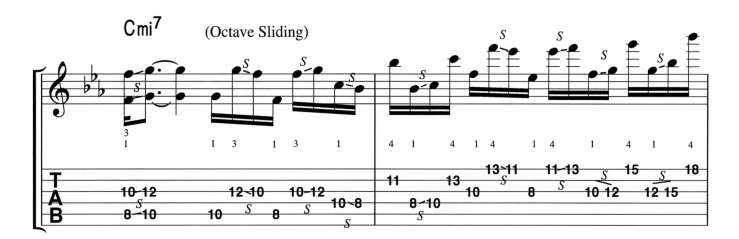

(Double Pentatonic String Skipping)

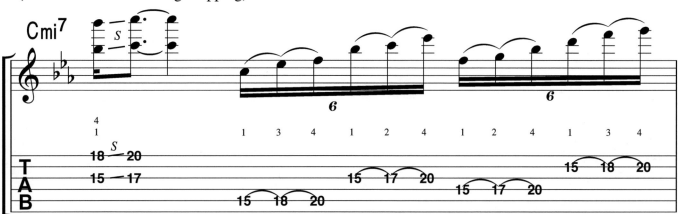

(Extended Arpeggio Run)

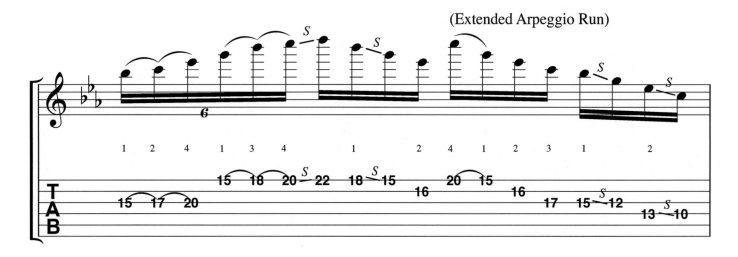

No. 28 ▸ Etude No. 5 (cont.)

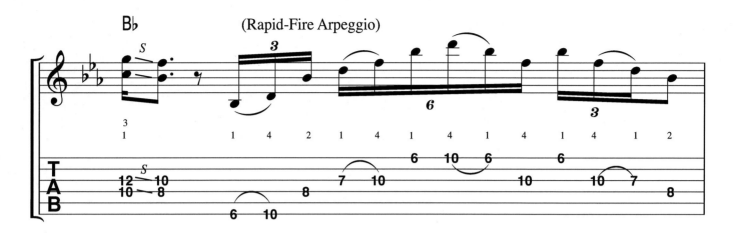

(Rapid-Fire Arpeggio)

(Hendrix Style Chord-Melody)

(Rapid-Fire Arpeggio)

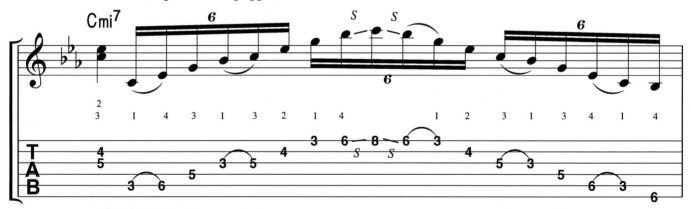

(Wide Interval Arpeggios)

No. 28 ▸ **Etude No. 5 (cont.)**

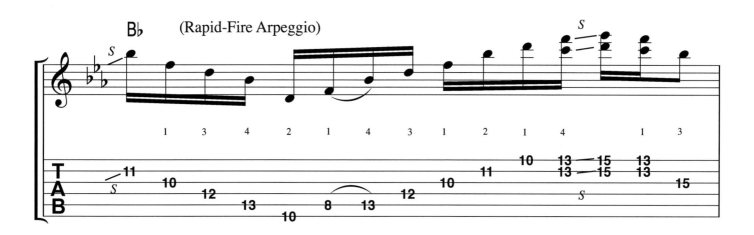

(Rapid-Fire Arpeggio)

(Horizontal Pentatonic Motion)

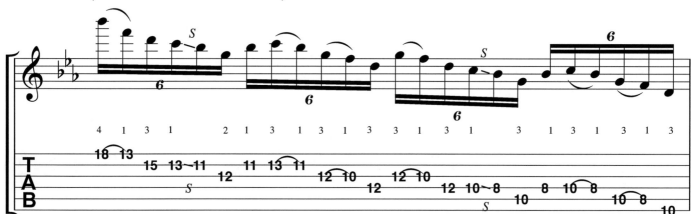

(Hendrix Style Chord-Melody)

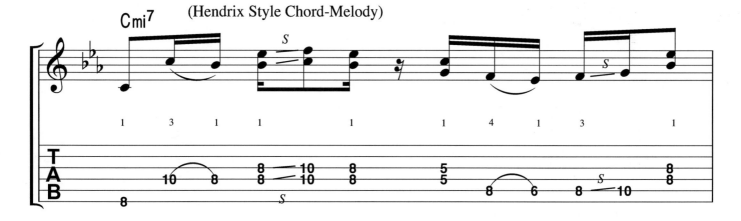

(Hendrix Style Chord-Melody)

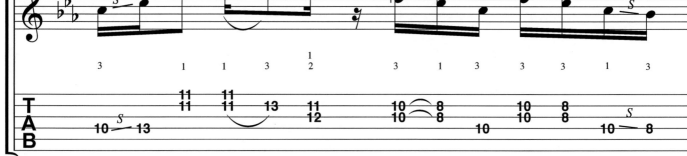

No. 28 ▸ Etude No. 5 (cont.)

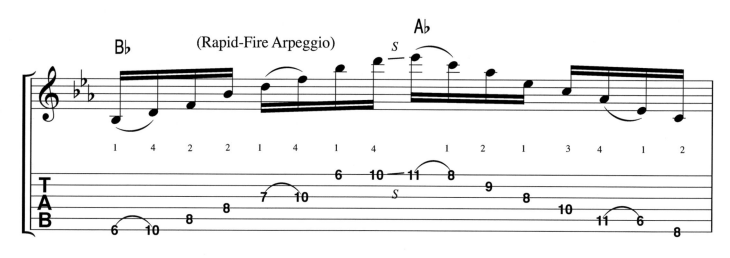

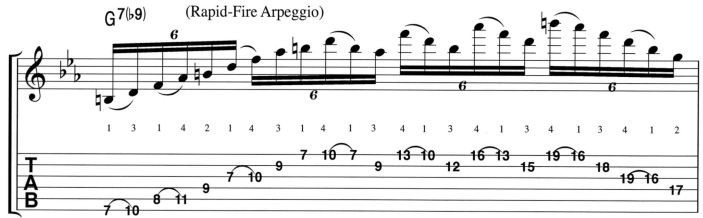

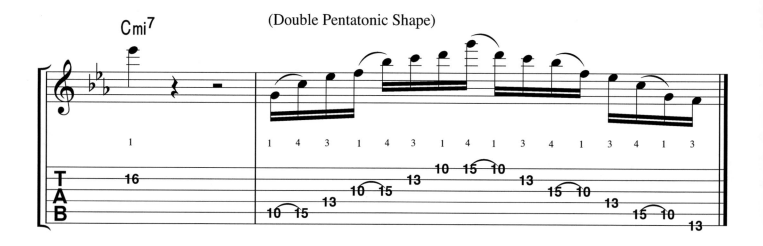

appendix

Guidelines for using this book

Developing Muscle Memory

Improvising with pentatonic chord-melody requires constant position shifting so as to avoid sounding repetitive. At its best, use of this technique flows across every nook and cranny of the fretboard, constantly exploring different ideas. This means the guitarist must be able to recall and execute a wealth of different moves and options. Virtuosic fretboard control is largely the result of muscle memory, when memorized finger patterns which are so familiar they can be played almost effortlessly. This gives a guitarist the mental freedom to listen to what he is playing and create music, rather than trying to continually remember where his fingers are supposed to go next.

In developing muscle memory, initial study and memorization should be very deliberate, with careful intellectual attention given to the execution of each and every note in a given study. First, memorize a study. Then, practice it frequently with a metronome at **ultra-slow speeds!** (as in one note-per-click with the metronome on 76 bpm)! While this may seem tedious, it will imprint the intellectual control of the pattern into your mind and hands. This slow-motion imprinting is crucial in developing fluidity and freedom, which will come later. It doesn't happen overnight, but rather over a period of months, as a particular pattern is practiced continually and carefully. Also, use this slow motion imprinting when practicing improvising with chord-melody. This will improve your continuity and execution of a wider variety of possible moves.

As you practice connecting passages at extremely slow tempos, practice looking ahead...to the next group of notes, even as your fingers are occupied with executing the notes of the moment. This is the psychological aspect of musicianship which is often overlooked and underdeveloped...the ability to focus the mental attention either directly on the notes of the moment, or to look ahead to the next group of notes mentally while the fingers rely on muscle memory to execute the notes of the moment. Consciously develop the mental habit of looking ahead to the upcoming group of notes. Memorize the studies herein and practice them in this way on a regular basis for a period of months, as this will assist in developing muscle memory.

Left-Hand Accuracy and Mental Concentration

In playing a given passage, pay close attention to notes that tend to be 'glitched'; that is, notes that don't sound fully with a ringing resonance. **You must be mindful and observant to pinpoint those notes that are not sounding fully, and then analyze the cause of the glitch.** This idea cannot be stressed enough. Take the time to observe and analyze the exact cause of the problem, on a given note, within a given exercise. Pentatonic chord-melody usually uses two notes at a time, often with a hammer-on, slide, or pull-off. Always make sure both notes sound fully, and be especially careful not to accidentally deaden the higher string being used when doing a hammer-on.

When working on a given exercise, learn to play it in slow motion, one section at a time. Be mindful not only of playing the notes evenly and continuously, but also of simultaneously keeping your body, hands, and mental attitude RELAXED! Pay close attention to the placement of each note. In this way, playing guitar is very much like the practice of meditation. While you strive to employ your will and intention to control the movements of your fingers, an inner tension naturally arises within your being as you strive to conquer a pattern. When working on new guitar movements, you should periodically remind yourself to relax...to mentally smile from within...to breathe deeply and calmly. Avoid having an attitude of striving to impress (yourself and/or others). Playing complex patterns on the guitar is truly a measure of your ability to concentrate. <u>Concentration translates to your ability to be focused and free from distraction as you play each note.</u> Distraction arises when you observe what you have just played, and then view it with pleasure or displeasure; or, when you start to think about someone else listening to you perform. This thought process should be released—let go of it. Instead, stay focused on the quality of your execution, on the quality of the sound of the notes.

Look inside a piano, and observe the precision with which each note is sounded. Each hammer, accurately playing each note at the desired moment. Let your fingers be like the hammers inside a piano. Disassociate your striving to play accurately from your emotional review of the results. Even if the notes are not entirely accurate, do not become bogged down in internal feelings of disappointment. And if the notes are performed accurately, do not focus on ideas of self-approval. Always stay focused on the craft, and release internal inclinations of self-approval or disappointment.

Final Wisdom

As you play an exercise slowly, use the imagery of the mechanical piano hammers. In fact, exaggerate the lifting and the independent abrupt placement of each finger, as if your fingers were like little hammers hitting the strings. It is a truly simple path, but many guitarists get sidetracked in their mental thought processes before they get around to solving the problem. Have the mentality of being a problem solver. Observe the execution of a difficult passage, playing it slowly with exaggerated left-hand finger placement. Analyze the cause of any glitched notes, and then adjust your hands accordingly. This may seem obvious, but it is actually a level of thinking that is more highly developed among virtuosos, rather than amateurs.

When working on a given pattern, memorize it so you can direct all of your visual and mental attention toward your hands and the guitar. Reading the exercise off the paper requires one third of your attention. Better to play a pattern from memory with eyes on the hands, thereby putting your mental energy into the execution of the passage, rather than into reading it.

Finally, be careful not to overstrain the left hand. During intense practice sessions, take timeouts to stretch the arms and hands. If you experience pain from continual and frequent playing, ease up. At that point, you should give your hands a rest for a couple days. To play guitar intensely for a lifetime, one must certainly be sensitive to the periodic pains and micro-injuries that may arise is the hands. These overuse pains (and even swellings) will often disappear if you reduce the intensity and frequency of your guitar playing, and immobilize your wrists and hands (for several days) with wrist braces, available at your local drugstore. Also, playing on a shorter scale length guitar neck (Gibson-style) as opposed to a longer scale length neck (Fender-style) puts a lot less strain on the left hand when working on patterns that require big stretches. That's because the frets are closer together on the short scale length guitar neck. When serious concerns arise with joints and tendons in the hands, do not hesitate in consulting a hand specialist doctor. Take care of your hands, so you can have a lifetime of playing guitar. As a lifetime career guitarist, this author speaks from experience. Now...get busy! (And don't forget to stretch gently.).

Tablature Symbols Key

Hammer-on	Pull-off	Slide	Grace Note

(Usually happens with a hammer or slide. It means the first note has no rhythmic value, and should be played abruptly and simultaneously with the target note, as a slight embellishment. Think of both notes rhythmically as one note.)

Check out the full series of these cutting-edge books
from Tim Quinn and Mel Bay Publications

The FLUID SOLOING SERIES by Tim Quinn

BOOK 1: Arpeggios for Lead Rock Guitar (MB20680BCD)
BOOK 2: Fluid Pentatonics for Guitar (MB20681BCD)
BOOK 3: Chord-Lead Soloing for Guitar (MB20679BCD)
BOOK 4: String Skipping and Wide-Interval Soloing (MB20682BCD)